Threefold Mary

Threefold *Mary*

by Emil Bock

WITH AN AFTERWORD BY
Michael Debus

TRANSLATED BY
Christiane Marks

SteinerBooks

This book is a translation of *Das dreifache Mariengeheimnis—Drei Vortrage, mit einem Nachwort von Michael Debus, published by Verlag Urachhaus © 1997 Verlag Freies Geistesleben & Urachhaus GmbH, Stuttgart, Germany. Translated by permission.*

Translation © Anthropsophic Press 2003

Published in the United States by SteinerBooks, P.O Box 799, Great Barrington, MA 01230
www.steinerbooks.org

Library of Congress Cataloging-in-Publication Data
Bock, Emil, 1895-1959.
[Dreifache Marien-geheimnis. English]
Threefold Mary / Emil Bock.-- 1st ed.
p. cm.
ISBN 0-88010-533-X
1. Mary, Blessed Virgin, Saint--Theology. 2.
Christengemeinschaft--Doctrines. I. Title.
BT613 .B6213 2003
232.91--dc22
2003019887

10 9 8 7 6 5 4 3 2 1

Printed in the United States

Contents

Preface

THIS LITTLE VOLUME contains three lectures delivered by Emil Bock at Christmas, 1950-51 under the title *The Mystery of the Virgin Mary in Spirit, Soul, and Body.* The first two were published in 1963-64 in the magazine *"Die Christengemeinschaft."* In revising the notes made during these lectures, though we have striven to create a readable text, we have taken equal care to preserve the quality of the spoken word. Therefore the lectures do not have the finish of a carefully formulated written text. Yet they seem so important, even today, that we are venturing to publish them in book form.

A hundred years after the 1854 dogma of the virgin birth, on November 1, 1950, Pope Pius XII proclaimed the dogma of the physical ascension, the bodily assumption into heaven, of the Virgin Mary. This event sent shock waves through all Christendom at the time. In his lectures Emil Bock tried to provide answers to some of the issues it raised. But he also expanded the subject considerably to describe not only the Mary-Sophia mystery in Christian history, but also the meaning and role of the feminine element in the development of human consciousness. In the process, he sheds new light on current questions and problems.

In his epilogue, written fifty years after these groundbreaking lectures were held, Michael Debus has added a theological overview of the development of the Marian theme in church history from early Christian times to the present. He gives us perspectives that carry us into the future, helping us to form a deeper, broader understanding of the mystery of the Virgin Mary.

—DR. GUNDHILD KAČER-BOCK

1

The Spiritual Aspect

THE CHRISTMAS FESTIVAL acts as a focal point in human life. It looks back to the past insofar as it commemorates the event that took place in Bethlehem 2,000 years ago. Since it recurs every year, however, Christmas is also linked to the present—though present-day consciousness cannot easily grasp the full significance of that. Children might sing carols like "The Christ Child Comes to Us Every Year," sensing that this yearly event belongs to the present, yet usually we are not aware of why this is so. Finally, there are also elements in our celebration of Christmas that reach into the future—both near and distant. This future-oriented element has significantly changed the mood in which we celebrate Christmas today. Consequently, the nostalgic mood of our childhood Christmases cannot be sustained unless new elements are added to those of the past. We will be able to understand the future content of the Christmas festival today only if as contemporary human beings we struggle to form truly understandable concepts of Christ's second coming in the supersensible—on the clouds of heaven. The second coming will not make our memories of his first coming and of the manger in Bethlehem superfluous, but it will be more powerfully relevant to the present. It is toward this second coming that we are inwardly growing. All the apocalyptic destinies of our time that are so foreign to the Christmas spirit, destroying its peace and making us look sadly upon the Christmas altar—"Peace on Earth"—all the apocalyptic shocks of the present age proclaim the approach of a new, future Christmas no longer centered on the lovely child but on *humanity*.

The Christian calendar itself indicates that Christmas contains the past, present, and future. December 24 is known as "Adam and Eve" day. Hence, at Christmas, we are not just looking back to Bethlehem, but farther back, as well, to humanity's beginnings in Paradise—the innocent beginnings gradually destroyed by the Fall. We could, in fact, call Christmas a variation on the theme of Paradise. I will discuss what I mean by that a little later. Finally, the day following the two days of Christmas— December 27—is consecrated to John the Evangelist, who was the author of the *Book of the Apocalypse*. John is the seer, who foretells the future. He is the herald of a future Christmas mystery. This day, then, points to the distant future.

Despite their simple humanity, the three figures gathered around the manger embody this universal principle. Old Joseph, the father, brings a great deal of the past to the scene. The child personifies the future. This leads us to ask, "What great mystery is expressed in the figure of Mary? How does she, the virgin mother, complete this threefold group around the manger? Which of our inner mysteries does she reflect back to us?" This lecture will try to show that the figure of the Virgin Mary has much to teach us both about the far-distant past and the far-distant future of human development. We may say that humanity is standing midway between two poles of salvation. Once closely joined to the divine world, we have now lost our connection with it—and with Paradise. The figure of Mary is a bodily reminder of this original closeness to God and the spiritual world. At the same time, she contains the first beginnings of fruits that will not ripen in us fully until our earthly journeys are complete. Therefore, as we talk about these things, let us try to see the figures around the manger in Bethlehem not only as memories of a historical event, but as figures in which we might be able to recognize ourselves in what we *no longer are* or what we have *not yet become.*

The figures around the manger are unique. They will never appear again in this form in human history. We may say that these figures descended from heaven and took on human shape. This is already a familiar process, because Christ came to us that way. We can picture it. Christ is a being at home in the most exalted spiritual regions who took on human shape. He took upon himself the burden of earthly incarnation. There were pre-Christian gods who died and returned to life, as well. Whether called Osiris in Egypt or Adonis in Phoenicia, the risen god was known and celebrated along with nature in seasonal cultic celebrations. Now this god, the one who dies and is resurrected, comes down from heaven and takes on human form.

Before that could happen, another being had to come down from heaven to earth. Mary in human shape mirrors this being, whom the ancient Egyptians called the goddess Isis, mother of the boy Horus. Isis was known by the world's peoples all the way to the Far East as the divine virgin mother. At the turning point of time, this image comes to us in the humblest human form. It came in the form of the virgin mother with the child in her arms, a young mother scarcely out of girlhood, who journeyed far from her native Nazareth to bear her child in a grotto in Bethlehem.

Two basic human mysteries confront us here. The first is the child in the manger, destined to grow up, go out into the world and through his resurrection vanquish what was known in mystery temples all over the world as the *mystery of death*. The other, the figure of Mary, personifies for us the *mystery of birth*. She is the goddess who gives birth and yet remains a virgin. That is the mystery at the other pole of human life.

Church history can be said to have lifted the human image of the ancient mother goddess back up to the heavens through the cult of Marian devotion. This, however, was not initiated until the height of the Middle Ages. From then on, the Madonna was worshiped as divine. Yet it is much more important to try to solve the mysteries of human life inherent in the figure of Mary than simply to declare her divine. Martin Luther and the other reformers sensed as much when they decided against making Marian devotion a part of Protestantism. They maintained that human beings, no matter how great the mysteries they might embody, should not be declared gods.

In the most recent past, more building blocks were added to the dogma of Marian devotion. In 1854, the Catholic Church proclaimed the dogma of the *conceptio immaculata*, the Immaculate Conception, to which in 1950 the dogma of the bodily ascension, the assumption into heaven of the Virgin Mary was added. Both dogmas effectively transfer to Mary a mystery connected to Christ, because this mystery swings like a pendulum between the miracles of the virgin birth and the assumption. It will become clearer during the course of this talk that the mystery of the virgin birth is a last echo of far distant Paradise, and that Christ's resurrection (which we are still learning to comprehend and share in more fully) still remains a distant goal for humankind.

First, however, we must strive with reverence to reapproach the divine mysteries in the life of the Virgin

Mary, using all the faculties of modern consciousness. Our maxim must be that our freedom as Christians depends on the extent to which we base our religious convictions on personal experience, on the extent to which we make creative use of the innermost core of our beings as we strive for a Christian understanding of the world. In this endeavor, we must continue to be the "revolutionaries" Christians have been from the beginning. We must strive for a Christianity that is continually reborn as it is quickened by insights growing from our free human consciousness.

One of the mysteries we must rediscover was known in pre-Christian times. It was the mystery that caused the earliest Christians in 1000 A.D. not to speak about the Virgin Mary at all, but to keep a tactful silence on the subject. She was never portrayed, either—there are no Western depictions of her prior to 1000 A.D. Not until the height of the Middle Ages, after the church had initiated Marian devotion, was she ever painted. The paintings created at that time were all those deeply intuitive portrayals we would not want to be without today, such as the ones by Raphael. But in early times, ecclesiastics as well as painters had reasons for not depicting the Madonna: They still knew of a Mary mystery too deep to be shown in painting. The high, holy mystery, which was too deep to speak about, involved the connection between the Virgin Mary and the Holy Spirit. She was, in fact, felt to be a personification of the Holy Spirit. In some areas of Austria and Bavaria we still find medieval depictions of the Trinity that show the Virgin Mary, instead of the Holy Spirit, alongside God the Father and Christ. That is an echo of this mystery. Now, we must in all honesty admit that there is probably no Christian concept more puzzling than that of the Holy Spirit. We find the Holy Spirit even harder to conceive of than Christ. To make any progress here, we must begin by trying patiently to recover the right concepts.

Loosely speaking, there are two aspects to the Holy Spirit. There is an ancient Holy Spirit and a new one; the Holy Spirit has its past and its future aspects. In the early stages of human development here on earth, referred to in the myth of Paradise, we were still at one with the Holy Spirit because our spiritual nature was not yet desecrated. The Fall had not yet corrupted and weakened the spirit. Originally, the Holy Spirit was active in an area that had been spared the effects of the Fall. In future, however, as humanity plunges deeper into sin, there must be a new Holy Spirit—and in fact it already exists as the healing spirit, the healer of sins, delivering and cleansing humanity after its fall into sin. The new Holy Spirit comes into being as our spiritual nature is cleansed of its corruption. This, in essence, is the original Christian concept of the Holy Spirit. Many more ancient pre-Christian mysteries impact Christianity than is commonly realized. As Christians, we must be aware of both aspects of the Holy Spirit— of the one not yet touched by the Fall and the one reversing the effects of the Fall through the healing of sins.

Looking back at the past, we see humanity naturally possessing an element of the Virgin Mary's nature, which is then lost by degrees. But we have not lost it entirely, not even today. Where in history do we encounter this natural Mary element poured out over humanity by the Holy Spirit in Paradise? Look at Mary sitting by the manger in Bethlehem. She is so indescribably ethereal, pure, and virginal because she embodies the heritage of Paradise. She shows us Paradise not yet lost—salvaged innocence kept alive for us since the first days of Creation.

Here we arrive at the subject of womanhood in general. It is impossible ever to stop marveling at the fact that a human being of flesh and blood should be able to give birth to another! This holy privilege of womanhood is often taken for granted, yet motherhood is the most exalted of miracles. Motherhood is a gift harking back to the time of original closeness to God. We still feel the aura of holiness surrounding a woman with child, yet we know that this emotion, this awareness, is in crisis. Humanity does not know how to guard and keep the holy gifts it has been given. Our materialistic age has brought with it a kind of thinking that leads us wholly into error. For example, the prevailing view is that virginity has been lost in a woman who conceives or has ever had contact with a man. This has blinded us to the fact that even today there are still many mothers who have not fully lost their virginal nature even after bearing children. On the other hand, there are countless unmarried women who perhaps have never had contact with a man and have lost their virginity. Coarse, crudely materialistic ideas have come up on this subject and caused the ever-present, universal mystery of the Virgin Mary to disappear from our culture.

The Mary mystery, insofar as it comes to us out of the past, still has its effects on women incarnated today. What is its nature? It lies in the fact that women do not incarnate in the same way as men. A woman's individual spirit, which is, of course, part of the entire spiritual world, is not joined to her the way a man's is. Due to the way a woman's being is organized, she feels her spiritual nature hovering above her. She is continually open in that direction. Today, however, many women have successfully "defeminized" themselves. Naturally, it is not those I am talking about here.

Let us remember that there is a cosmic symbol for the feminine nature. At a certain stage, pre-Christian religions connected the mystery of Mary to the earth itself, which is why, even today, we still speak of "Mother Earth." Remember the original divine hierarchy of the Greeks. Their main gods were Gaia and Uranos, Earth and Heaven. Gaia was the symbol of the earth before its tragic separation from the spiritual world had begun. Gaia and Uranos, the divine pair, ruled the world. Then, the Greek myth continues, they had a son, Chronos, who killed his father.

Earth then entered into a relationship with heaven resembling that of a widow with her deceased husband. This Greek myth speaks to us specifically of the mysteries of womanhood that reach back deep into the past to the original gifts bestowed on humanity at creation.

The Biblical account of creation begins this way: Earth existed, but it was still in a flowing state, and the spirit of God hovered over the waters. This image holds true for human beings, as well as for the earth. At first we did not have the sturdy skeleton we have today. Our bodies were much more fluid and malleable. Therefore, we could just as well say, "The spirit hovered over humanity." Women have in part preserved this stage of creation to the present day. In men, everything entered the bones. The spiritual fully entered into the physical. In sexual difference we have a symbol that must be read carefully. It can teach us that in men it is primarily the earthly sphere that speaks, while in women, to a certain degree, heaven still speaks, reminding us of humanity's original, heaven-surrounded state. That is why woman still has this wonderful mandate to create as nature creates, especially in her plant kingdom. Plants, of course, still live entirely in a state of cosmic innocence. But if humanity did not also retain the last traces of this innocence, then all women would have become barren long ago.

Looking back to the very earliest days of human history, we come upon a very remarkable fact. Even the historians of the last few centuries have been able to discover it. The very earliest cultures were guided by women. In the beginning, we do not find patriarchies but matriarchies, where women are the community leaders. What does this tell us? The primacy of women rests on the fact that, by her very nature, woman was open to the spirit. Old Testament myths are in conflict with this outlook. The Old Testament stems from a strongly male spiritual stream that neglects the mystery of the feminine. Following the biblical myths back far enough, of course, we do come to feminine leadership—but Eve is considered responsible for plunging humanity into sin. According to the prevailing view, it was woman who brought evil into the world. Adam only went along with her. On this point, we need to change our thinking completely. The new interpretation will not take away from the tragedy of the Fall. On the contrary, it will make it plainer.

Let us begin by asking, "Why was Eve created in the first place?" How shall we answer? You may say, "Well, it was so that humanity could reproduce." But that is not so, because there was a kind of reproduction before Eve existed. Today, of course, when we think of reproduction, we think of sexual reproduction. Therefore, we imagine that Adam, the man, existed first and then Eve was molded from his flesh. But it is a serious error to think that man existed first and woman came later. For Adam is not *man*, but the first *human being*. The human being was created first.

The creation passage in Genesis really reads, "God created a human being, male-female." This was misunderstood to mean God created a man and a woman. The fact that the creation of Eve is not mentioned until much later points up this misunderstanding. The first human being, Adam, was both man and woman, male and female, and thus capable of reproducing in a way that was a part of original Creation. Guided by higher beings, this human being could sacrifice a part of its nature out of which would grow the beginnings of a body that would receive another human soul. This was virgin birth, since the bisexual human being was capable of reproduction. But we must not imagine that this human being looked like us and had bones, limbs, and sensory organs like ours. Above all, it still lacked that primary human characteristic, upright posture. At that time, humans had only rudimentary physical bodies. Today's lower sea animals may here and there remind us of those early human beings who were not yet fully incarnated and whose bodies were not yet quite physical. Such are the beings the biblical Creation myth speaks of. Of course we must remember that back then their physical surroundings would have been quite different, too.

What I have outlined here stands many accustomed ideas and concepts on their heads. At the same time, it is the beginning of a renewed understanding of humanity. So the means of reproduction existed before the sexes were separated, and Eve was not just created in order to bear children. She was created for conception in the widest sense—to conceive, to receive, everything that heaven was sending down to earth. Before the Fall, Eve conceived the Holy Spirit because the spirit was then still in its original hallowed state. The existence of woman after the separation of the sexes made it possible for humanity to conceive the Holy Spirit. Man, who was not suitable for this role, was given other tasks. Eve's first son, Cain, was conceived the old way, not sexually, but in the old, pure way, under the direction of the spiritual world.

A misunderstanding of the biblical creation story is largely responsible for the fact that the word "conception" has become so narrow in its meaning. Today, "conception" is defined as that moment in sexual union when motherhood first begins. That is not accurate. This phenomenon of sexual union only plays a helping role, giving nature a boost, since our human nature has been moving toward sterility for tens of thousands of years now. What does a woman conceive when she becomes a mother? She conceives a being of spirit and soul, which hovers over her and then approaches her, taking up its abode in the body she is preparing in her womb. This is the true process of conception. It is, however, preceded by physical preparation, purely physiological processes lasting about eighteen days. Not until these have been completed does true conception occur. It is then that the spirit and soul of the child coming down to earth unite with the budding physical body in the womb. Long ago, when most people still had higher vision, they could see the soul and spirit of the incarnating child. Mothers on the point of conception, in particular, were able to see their child. In early times, today's crude, even soulless ideas on this subject would have been unthinkable. These ideas have already done tremendous harm because our materialistic interpretation emphasizes the secondary elements. The real event has been forgotten. Yet it is this very event that we must learn to focus on again if we are to come to any sort of understanding of the mystery of the Virgin Mary.

Basically, the process of conception by which a woman becomes a mother is no different from that through which she became the bearer of the spirit in the earliest days of history. Spirit then approached the human world. Woman—Eve, before the Fall—was able to receive it. That is why, in the Old Testament myth, Eve is able to see and hear the supersensible being that has come to entice Adam and Eve and lead them astray. Adam is not able to hear it—Eve is ahead of him here. Woman is able to conceive, that is, to cognize, to receive knowledge, on the purely spiritual level and also on the level of spirit and soul. What is thus taken in penetrates more deeply—deeply enough to enter the embryo in the womb. The process of childbearing and that of cognition, of receiving knowledge, are therefore closely linked, which is why in old times "begetting" was spoken of as "knowing."

Outer research cannot tell us about earliest times, because there are no documents. But spiritual researchers are able to look back in the spirit and to read the cosmic script that preserves in readable form traces of all that ever happened on earth. It is in this script, the Akasha Chronicle, that Rudolf Steiner tells us about earliest human history in *Cosmic Memory*.[1] He gives a particularly vivid account of the process by which humanity moved from a dream state to a first rudimentary consciousness, and by means of that to cultural life: Let us follow Rudolf Steiner back to the Lemurian period, far back into the earth's past, to a time when human bodies had not "crystallized out" or defined their shape the way they have today. Rudolf Steiner relates that during that period male and female children were brought up differently. The male children were prepared for a life of will and action. The development of their outwardly active side was emphasized. Female children, on the other hand, were guided in quite a different direction. Their earliest education was designed solely to develop their imagination. Young girls were led to places where they could observe the forces of nature at work—in storms, for example—or men fighting or engaging in other acts of will. Here we must remember that eyes such as ours did not yet exist; and yet, in some fashion, these young girls were made to witness events that had an element of drama to them. And in perceiving these, their imagination began to develop, generating images, laying the first founda- tions for human consciousness. But Rudolf Steiner states clearly that it was impossible for this process to lead to wildly fantastic or deviant thoughts, because at this stage humanity did not yet have memory. "The dreamlike or dramatic images merely crossed the soul and disappeared along with the outer stimulus causing them. So they were based on sound outer reality, never sinking into quagmires."

Consciousness and the ability to dream, deliberately developed, formed the basis for memory; the dreamers began to be able to remember some of their dreams and, after that, to be able to compare and make choices, to distinguish between what was useful to them and what wasn't. Rudimentary memory also made possible the formation of the first moral concepts—the ability to distinguish good and evil—which led to the beginnings of a legal system. Customs, moral codes, came into being. Step by step, human consciousness opened up to the world. And it was always woman who developed these new attributes, because hers was the role of conception/reception. "All who strive for a true understanding of human development must be aware that the first strides in imagining, in the creation of inner images, were made by women. They are the ones who first thought, imagined and remembered, and that is a prerequisite for the formation of memory. Memory, in turn, made possible the development of habits, and habits laid the foundation for a legal code, a kind of framework of custom and morality. It was man who knew and dealt with the forces of nature, but it was woman who first interpreted them."

Man stood squarely in the midst of natural forces, which determined his actions. Woman, meanwhile, began to develop understanding of these forces. Rudolf Steiner goes on to say that this understanding enabled women to purify and ennoble the still-unbridled forces in men. When women and girls began learning to imagine, remember, and unfold their inner lives at this early stage of consciousness, they were still in quite a dreamlike state and did not yet think at all the way we do. Images moved through their souls as dreams do in sleep. The women fell into a kind of trance, yet this was a state in which they could have these waking dreams. And while they were in this state, nature sent them messages from the spiritual world. As women perceived the spirit that formed a part of their surroundings, as they grew to love and revere the higher spiritual beings, religion was born. Women were the priests because they were the ones who could create the connection with the spiritual world. Men depended on, and were nurtured by, the spiritual life of women.

Finally, language began to form, because the spiritual world, during those earliest times, was filled with sounds, which even the ancient Greeks still heard and called the music of the spheres. The cosmic word resounded and murmured throughout the world. The emotions of the women opened more and more to the word-like forces moving through their souls, seeking to enter their consciousness; a kind of nature language began to form. "The inner rhythms of nature sounded from the lips of 'wise' women. People gathered around them, feeling the chanted phrases to be the communications of higher powers. Gatherings such as these were the first religious services."

But Rudolf Steiner states quite clearly that these phrases were not taken in like thought, but like music. Human language grew out of divine language in the form of sung words. Woman was the first to be able to conceive/receive like this and passed what she had conceived on to the man. A kind of liturgy was created out of the ancient wise women's sung words by the people gathered about her, and gestures began to accompany the chanting.

In this way, imagination, memory, custom and morality, religion, liturgy, music and language were formed, in that order. Women conceived all these things. Women passed these accomplishments on to the rest of humanity. This is what lies behind the historical phenomenon of matriarchy in ancient times. In the Biblical myth, it was Eve's intelligence that led her to disobey and eat the fruit of the tree of knowledge, but this also enabled her to distinguish between right and wrong, and without this faculty there could never have been any cultural life. It was a necessary step in human development, even though it brought on the tragedy of the Fall, initiating ever greater separation from God. In the earliest days of human history, wisdom—Sophia—came to life in the souls of women. The earliest divine revelations, intended to sustain humanity on its journey, came by way of women.

It is important to be aware that the Fall affects different human functions at different rates. Here we have two of these functions: First, cognition, from the outset a capacity of woman since woman is the one who conceives, who takes in spiritual truths. Second, the process of birth, of reproduction. Reproduction is just an intensification, a metamorphosis of cognition. It is simply a completion on the physical level of what happens in cognition. This is humanity's primal condition. The human journey began with the Holy Spirit, but through the Fall, humanity lost its holiness. At the same time, cultural leadership passed from woman to man. As a result of the Fall, woman's ability to conceive the spirit grew decadent, and the spirit was masculinized. This constituted a transition from heavenly knowledge to earthly knowledge, Today's materialistic way of thinking is the last stage of our fall into sin as it affects our cognition. Earthly thinking is still relatively young, because supersensible perception existed well into historic times.

Similarly, the innocence of Paradise, the conception of truth through the Holy Spirit, will still continue to echo in our culture for some time, as will the innocent virgin birth. Originally, the physical part of sexual union was not perceived. It occurred entirely on the unconscious level, so that spiritual conception was what mattered—conception from the world in which the child's soul and spirit originated. The mystery of the virgin birth was once common to all of humanity; it was not lost until the Fall led us deeper and deeper into sin. And we see in the young girl from Nazareth, in Mary's young, pure, and still heavenly, holy soul the possibility of recapturing what humanity lost tens of thousands of years ago. In Mary, Paradise is fully present on earth once more. Nowhere in the Bible does it say anything about a fatherless birth, and those within the Catholic church who know about these things never say "fatherless birth," either, but instead, *conceptio immaculata*. The view that the birth took place without the participation of a father did not come up until conception had started to mean only the sexual part of the process. This view grows out of the materialism of our age. The virgin birth of the child Jesus takes place in Mary. The Catholic Church has now traced this fact back to Mary's parents. We know that the Mary described in the Gospel of Luke came from the simple Nazarene community where her parents would still have had this innocence, too. Modern theology considers the parents of the Luke Gospel Mary to be Joachim and Anna, but they are really the parents of the other Mary, the one described in the Gospel of Matthew; the two should not be confused. Joachim and Anna conceive under somewhat different circumstances, harking back in a way to ancient times, when this was occasionally possible: Like Abraham and Sara, they have children at an age when nature usually no longer allows it. This is another form of *conceptio immaculata* left over from the age of Paradise.

Cognition, the process of learning, becomes increasingly masculine as the effects of the Fall deepen.

In the process, it also ceases to be virginal, and spirituality—spiritual and cultural life today—is no longer of the Holy Spirit, either in the ancient or in the modern sense. Spirituality has become earthly— the spirit has become the unholy spirit, which, in fact, evolves into the evil spirit. Many people feel that their thoughts still have spiritual content, but, due to the nature of their thinking, they are injuring and continually destroying the spirit. Today's souls are no longer worthy vessels for spiritual matters. The spiritual no longer penetrates us. The patriarchy, the primacy of men, which replaced the original matriarchy, has been with us for thousands of years now, as a necessary stage of our development. Of course, we cannot return to bygone times, but we have to see clearly today that the narrow masculinization of our entire culture has caused women to put on men's clothing and think in masculine terms, as well, so they are no longer able to make their particular contribution to spiritual and cultural life. This profound cultural problem cannot be solved simply by allowing women to serve as ministers—and subordinate ones, at that—as the Protestant church is doing more and more. Today, a much more important question is this—how can we return to what is truly human? How can we, as human beings, regardless of sex, create and support culture?

To many of us today, the Holy Spirit is nothing more than a phenomenon of ecstatic religious experience. But if humanity is to reapproach the mystery of the Holy Spirit, there will have to be basic changes in cognition, in the way we think and understand. Religion and everything associated with it has been so far removed from thinking that it does not occur to anyone that the Holy Spirit might have anything to do with thinking at all. Actually, it should be associated with thinking first and foremost. All of humanity must regain the power of spiritual conception, which used to be the privilege of women. We may be sure that after a few decades there will be many who can begin again to perceive the supersensible in the world, or at least to feel it, to sense it. Truly, when that point is reached, we will no longer see just the material aspects of outer nature that the masculine brain speculates on, but we will see the spiritual along with them. When that point is reached, our souls will again conceive thoughts the way a woman conceives and bears a child. Goethe took the first few steps in that direction in giving us guidelines toward a kind of thinking that is not just abstractly added onto what the senses perceive. In this kind of thinking, thought and perception enter into a union, a marriage of heaven and earth.

In the Acts of the Apostles (I:14) we read that Mary is present when, on Pentecost morning, the first congregation and the disciples receive the Holy Spirit. Now it is no longer only the woman, but also the eleven disciples, along with the others gathered about her; to whom fate has granted the gift of experiencing the spirit as it enters our sphere to make spiritual cognition strong and fruitful again. Mary is one of them; thus it is often shown in paintings. We will just keep this image in mind for now. It has special meaning for the Christian Community, insofar as we are dedicated to ordaining women as well as men to our priesthood.

All women will come to appreciate the fact that there are female priests, that women are able to reopen our souls to the spirit in a way that is appropriate for today. Beyond that, all humanity, including men, must welcome into this cognitive life the principle of the eternal feminine, which has nothing to do with the difference between man and woman. As carrier of the historic Holy Spirit, the mystery of the Virgin Mary must be renewed with the Holy Spirit of today. Our souls must be opened to the spiritual world and spiritual truths in such a way that cognition is reverential conception of what the spirit gives us. When Christianity really takes effect in human thinking, then there will be wisdom on earth again. That is the spiritual aspect of the mystery of the Virgin Mary, its age-old pre-history, and the way it must be regained on a new level.

2

The Soul Aspect

LET US FOCUS our inner eye again on the image of the childlike virgin mother, Mary, attending her baby in the manger. This mother is more than a woman of flesh and blood who lived on earth 2,000 years ago. There is a timeless quality to her in which we must try to find the reflection of our own higher being.

Now, let us turn our gaze to a variation, a different form, of the Christmas theme. It is found at the end of the New Testament. The image is not idyllic and filled with heavenly peace like that of Bethlehem. Here, the heavens are torn open as the spiritual worlds reveal the image of a woman of majestic size. Clothed in the sun, she stands on the moon and wears the stars for a crown. This woman is about to bear her little son. But mother and child are in danger. The dragon lies in wait. A battle is breaking out in heaven. The archangel Michael and his legions are defending the mother and child against the dragon's powers. Here we have an apocalyptic Christmas scene, contrasting sharply with the peaceful, lyrical scene described in the Gospel of Luke.

But—we must ask—what do these two women have to do with each other? Is it even permitted to juxtapose them, and call both scenes "Christmas images"? It might be helpful here to supplement Luke's Christmas scene with the one described in the Gospel of Matthew. In Matthew, too, we have the mother and child, but under threat, like the Mary of the Apocalypse. The dragon has taken on human form in Herod, who represents the threat to mother and child. There is as yet no need for the archangel's legions, but the three wise men, those noble protectors and helpers, have the authority to thwart his intentions. And the angel who appears to Joseph in a dream is able to save the child by directing his parents to flee to Egypt.

Thus we see that the first hints of apocalyptic drama are already present in the Gospel account of the Christmas story. As we place the peaceful and the apocalyptic Christmas images side by side, we become aware that today we are making the transition from the one to the other. Actually, we are already quite close to the second. In future, the idyllic Christmas scene described by Luke, and the Mary mystery that forms a part of it, will come only to those who have already endured the firestorms of the apocalyptic Christmas event. They will have learned to see the divine mother figure as the image of their own souls and the child about to be born to her as the spirit growing and coming to life within them. In future, we will not be able to find our way back to the idyllic Luke Christmas experience and the Mary mystery as a part of it until we have gone through the trials and firestorms of the apocalyptic image. In those storms, we must first learn to see the heavenly mother as an image of our soul. We must learn to see the spirit child in her womb and about to be born as an image of our own budding spirit. We will be able to find our way back to the serene inwardness of the Luke Christmas account only by way of the apocalyptic image. When we do, we will possess it on a higher level. But first we must lose this ancient Christmas of the soul entirely. Today we can no longer simply see the virgin mother as an image of the human soul, and the little child on her lap or in the manger as an image of the spirit growing within us. Soul and spirit, mother and child, are threatened precisely because humanity has lost the mystery of the spirit.

Humanity has become tremendously clever, but is entirely lacking in wisdom. Our brains are full of abstract constructs. Spirit is not what it used to be and still should be. It has become an evil spirit. Our souls are half dead from the onslaught of the chill, the frost, of thinking that lacks all soul. Souls can no longer produce warmth or love, because the little bit of life they still have is continually consumed in struggling to survive the frosty winds blowing over them out of the heads and hearts of others. How can we bring the mystery of the Virgin Mary to life again?

We have looked back to the time when the original Marian revelations were not yet used up, when the spirit light humanity received from the bosom of God before the Fall still shone. But then came the transition from the feminine to the masculine principle of cognition. Cognition was no longer in the hands of those who were open to the divine, but of those who were enclosed in the earthly sphere. When the gift of heaven faded, and thinking and cognition grew ever more earthbound, Christian leaders grew alarmed at what might become of human thought in the future. One of the most important historical turning points occurred here, one that brought basic changes to the face of central Europe: Out of undefinable depths came the urge to fell the great forests and start building cities. These cities were surrounded by open, light-bathed pastures and fields of grain. People who had previously lived in the quiet and isolation of the forest now lived together in big cities. This strong, sudden cultural impulse, which occurred around 1200, came out of an inner human awakening. A new spiritual capacity was struggling to be born. Humanity could no longer remain in the dreamy sphere of feeling. People had to rub the sleep from their eyes and, awakening, take a very specific step: Using the terms coined by Rudolf Steiner, we may say humanity had to step out of the "sentient soul" into the "consciousness soul." The human soul had give birth to a capacity to receive the spirit. The sudden impulse to found a new kind of culture was the outer expression of this inner development. Seemingly overnight, the culture of the cities and the bourgeoisie appeared. In the beginning, city building was still steeped in the patriarchal element, but through awakened thinking, through the developing consciousness soul, humanity grew into a totally new state—that of individual freedom. At the same time, there were losses. Awakening intellect now regards heaven less, focusing more and more on worldly things. Where will this ultimately lead?

In the previous century the cultural stream that Rudolf Steiner called "arabism" flowed up into Europe from the east and south. It brought with it an extreme intellectualism—a narrow, brain-bound intelligence—and demonstrated what the intellectual development of city dwellers and the increasing secularization of life were bound to lead to. It opened a first window on the ice age of the soul. The church took numerous steps at this point in cultural history—around 1200—in order to minimize the danger. It founded the great monastic orders, the mendicant Franciscan and Dominican orders, to counteract these future developments. The same desire to defend humanity against the new dangers gave rise to Gothic architecture. Previously, when forests still dominated the landscape, Romanesque cathedrals and churches were built, which, in their crystalline solidity and darkness, were still wholly an expression of the mystery of the incarnation of the divine in earthly matter. Romanesque architecture was replaced overnight by Gothic. Structures soared high, topped with slender spires, high pillars, finials and little decorative towers that rose up everywhere among the windows and roofs. The direction is not that of incarnation, from above downwards. Religion is now drawn forth from the human soul, portrayed as the uprising longing for heaven.

This was also the time when Marian devotion officially began—at least, in recent history. The mystery of the Virgin Mary had already been known, but it was not spoken of. The close relationship between the mystery of the Holy Spirit and that of the Virgin Mary, particularly, was very well known, and cosmic wisdom, Sophia, was sensed behind the figure of Mary. Mary was like a window on heaven, giving us glimpses of the riches waiting there, to be continually bestowed on the faithful like Christmas gifts. People felt that good thoughts and artistic inspiration flowed from this cosmic wisdom. But this knowledge was bound to fade when Marian cognition, which was still a kind of conception—with every thought being taken in on a spiritual level—was succeeded by abstract, intellectual thinking. It was at this point that Marian devotion was officially inaugurated and given an important place. This was because the church foresaw a great future danger in the removal of soul from nature and from all life by increasingly narrow, intellectual thinking. So, as a counterweight, the symbol of the soul was placed at the center of religious life. This was also the point at which a whole treasury of Madonna paintings was created and numerous churches were dedicated to Mary. The figure of Mary suddenly became like a watchword of the church. This development is understandable, and it is possible to affirm it, as indeed we need to affirm every historical event. But at the same time, we must not fail to see the tragic consequences that followed. The church had inaugurated an impulse to strengthen the soul at the expense of spiritual development. Spirit and soul were severed because only the soul was emphasized in religious life. The spirit became more and more secularized and intellectualized. And after human cognition and thinking were, in effect, left out of the religious realm and no longer enjoyed the warm sheltering mantle of religion, weren't they bound to become cold and soulless all the faster?

Several events preceded the era of Marian devotion, preparing the groundwork for the developments just described. The most important of these was the Council of Constantinople of 869. This council decreed the human being to consist only of body and soul. What is commonly called "spirit" is not really part of the human body; it just overshadows it. That is how the church arrived at the dogma that human beings consist of body, soul, and certain spiritual capacities. The triad, the three-note chord of body, soul, and spirit, was lost in this official church teaching, according to which human beings no longer possessed spirit as the most important member of their being. From that time on, humanity was said to consist only of body and soul.

This was a first indication of the fact that the new spiritual phenomenon of brain-bound, narrowly intellectual thinking would not be acknowledged to be spiritual in nature at all. Let us reflect for a moment on how this must have affected attitudes toward the Virgin Mary. Since ancient times, Mary, the prototype of the human soul, had been considered to be the bearer of the Holy Spirit. When the church dogmatically claimed that human beings consist only of body and soul, it followed that the faithful would begin to consider Mary as nothing but soul, soon forgetting that this pure, heavenly image, the virgin mother, is a window on the Holy Spirit that longs to be received by all humanity. As beneficial as Marian devotion was, it placed soul before spirit, covering and obscuring the spiritual aspect of Mary. This caused the Holy Spirit/Mary Mystery to be totally forgotten.

In addition, Marian devotion was inaugurated as a bulwark against some new impulses arising in humanity. The church was not at all inclined to allow the development of the I-strengthening soul capacity known as the "consciousness soul." It did not want to see humanity grow out of the childlike dependency that had been proper and justified in earlier times.

From a certain point of view, the truth of the dogma of 869 cannot be disputed. It is true—in a way—that only body and soul incarnate today. But that does not mean that we possess only body and soul. What it does mean is that we have not yet been able to incarnate our spiritual selves, which are still hovering "over" us. Men easily forget this, and because, for all time to come, it is over women that this spirit self will continue to hover—as "over the waters of creation"—it behooves women to keep the knowledge alive. But we must realize today that human beings are more "themselves" in what they have not yet become than in what they now are. It is what hovers over us that makes up our true being. It would be depressing, indeed, if our outer bodies running around over this earth today were our true selves! Our true being is still a thing of the future. In spite of its relative accuracy, the dogma of 869 has done grave harm in conveying the impression that we are only what we have already become. This is the consequence of the church's actions. The doors *must* be left open to allow humankind to go on growing and progressing, developing and incarnating more and more fully. The tragic aspect of Marian devotion as proclaimed at that particular point in history is that, ironically, the holy symbol of the virgin mother Mary was used to confine human beings to their soul aspects, to arrest their progress at the soul level, at the expense of their spiritual development.

Another historical event is directly connected with developments following the inauguration of Marian devotion: One of the greatest thinkers of that century—the century in which cities were founded—

was Thomas Aquinas. He is known and admired for praying to the Virgin Mary for divine help and inspiration when pursuing his theological studies. This clearly shows that the great minds of that time still knew of the spiritual mystery connected with Mary. They still knew the sources of spiritual inspiration and wisdom. On the other hand, though, Thomas Aquinas saw the need to make a distinction that had the most fateful consequences for the development of Christian thought: He stated clearly what his contemporaries also knew or thought they knew, teaching the distinction between truths arrived at by thought and those stemming from revelation. Human reason is limited, and truth that comes to us by revelation cannot be arrived at by reason or thinking. This distinction casts a dark, tragic shadow over the bright light of scholastic wisdom, for it is from the separation between reasoned truth and revealed truth that the separation of faith and knowledge grew. And this separation allowed religious thought and scientific research and study to grow farther and farther apart. The unity of spiritual and cultural impulses was lost. And it was inevitable that the Virgin Mary should be placed on the side of faith, where she could no longer be the patron saint of thinking and the source of wisdom.

The Fall is not a momentary, one-time event in the distant past, but a long process that allows certain human functions and capacities to fall gradually from their original sphere. The two most important human capacities, formerly closely joined, have been effected more and more deeply by the Fall. They are the process of cognition, by means of which the spirit conceived when things still proceeded according to God's will, and the process of birth, which depends on woman's unique gift to conceive the spirit even into the physical realm, and to give birth to it. In Christian thought there has been too little attention paid to the fact that cognition, the whole process of understanding, of gaining knowledge, has been corrupted by the Fall. The Fall and our ensuing sinfulness are normally associated exclusively with moral issues: Humanity has become corrupt, sinful, enslaved to sensuality, and so forth. Yet it is our present way of thinking that is the primary sin. The way we think separates us from God and causes us to fall from the divine sphere. Our moral fall is only an inevitable consequence of the fall of our cognitive process. When the spirit ceases to uphold us, it is no wonder that we fall in our moral nature.

In pre-Christian times, the heavenly, divine power—the world soul, which continually receives the Holy Spirit and is therefore the bearer of wisdom—was called "Isis Sophia." Sophia, of course, means "wisdom." The name "Sophia" was dropped and Isis remained, finally becoming Venus. The ancient goddess of wisdom becomes the goddess of a kind of love no longer pure as Paradise, but fallen to the level of sensuality. When Marian devotion was initiated and the spiritual side of Mary was being increasingly lost and only the soul aspect remained, Mary was looked on as an Isis who had not become Venus. The faithful saw in her the purity of Paradise preserved, untouched by the Fall, and never entangled in earthly snares.

But this virgin mother in Bethlehem did not have to struggle to maintain her purity. She is the only soul in world history in which the innocence of Paradise was preserved in spite of universal descent into sin. Hers is the primal innocence to which we cannot return. That is why contemplation of the Virgin Mary could never be anything but nostalgic longing for Paradise lost. The image of Mary could not help decisively in our own struggle for purification, purity of soul. Then what is it that can help cleanse the human soul, making it pure and innocent again? Moral resolutions and vows of chastity never help. The only way to renewed purity and radiance of soul is to allow the spirit to radiate through that soul. The spirit might still be hovering over us, not yet in our possession, but it is still able to bring light to the hearts whose warmth has become close and oppressive. Humanity will only be purified and raised to a higher state as spiritual forces permeate our souls. Anthroposophists call this process the creation of the "spirit self" or "Manas." This means that through the agency of the spirit, our souls develop a new member—the pure Marian soul. And the tragedy is that Marian devotion has been relegated to an area that could be called "for soul only," which places us in the same predicament as Baron von

Münchhausen stuck in the swamp, convinced that he will be able to pull himself out by his own pigtail. That is simply impossible. And so it is precisely Marian devotion that necessarily has given rise to a somewhat selfish religious attitude. Once the theology behind the movement had emphasized the "soul only" [*nur Seele*] aspect, souls began to say to themselves, "If I could only find blessedness [*Seligkeit*] and forgiveness of my sins!" There are still Christian traditions, particularly in Protestantism and various sects, that do not count on the spiritual world at all, but struggle ceaselessly and hopelessly with the problem of sin while trying to develop some conception of Christ or Mary that might be helpful in that struggle.

The word *Seligkeit* ["blessedness or bliss"] is quite remarkable. In German, *selig sein* [to be in a state of blessedness or bliss] originally meant quite simply to be ensouled, to have a soul, to be human and endowed with soul. But the word later developed emotional nuances, and has come to denote religious ecstasy. We could say it refers to soul without spirit, the soul as an end in itself—that is, feeling one's own soul in such a way as to experience bliss.

Let us find New Testament passages containing expressions like *selig werden* [to attain blessedness or bliss] or *selig machen* [to make blessed or beatify]. Martin Luther's translation is not at all faithful to the original here. Where Luther says, "The Son of Man has come to bring blessedness/bliss [*selig zu machen*] to those who were lost," the Greek text says *sozein,* and this simply means "to heal." The noun is *sotér*, the physician, the healer. So the Bible itself is much more objective here. It's not a matter of giving the soul bliss [*der Seele Seligkeit zu geben*] but of healing it of its sickness. That is a totally different matter. "To attain bliss" is always *sothénai* in Greek—"to be healed." The self-centered desire for personal bliss is truly a part of Marian devotion. Mary was worshipped as an intercessor, an aid in achieving longed-for personal bliss. Traces of this attitude can even be found in a spiritual movement influenced by Rosicrucianism, represented here by Angelus Silesius:

I must be Mary and give birth to God within.
That is the way in which he grants his bliss.

Angelus Silesius was a member of the ancient Christian wisdom tradition that did not go along with church dogma, and neither did he, though he was a Catholic. But he, too, says, "That is the way in which he grants his bliss," and his verse ends in the realm of mere soul. But we do not strive to be Mary and give birth to God within to assure our own bliss. We do so in order that the divine might have any influence in the world at all, and so that heaven and earth are not torn apart for good. We ourselves are not so important here, but, to be sure, we will feel the effects of bliss/healing [*des Heils*] also.

But Marian devotion has brought forth a wealth of beauty, too. How poor the Christian world would be if we did not have our treasure trove of Madonna paintings, the holiest, most beautiful of which were created by Raphael! These paintings go beyond showing us images of the girl of Nazareth; they also capture the timeless heavenly image revealed to us through her human countenance. The Madonna painters saw before them a heavenly being not identical with a human being who lived in Palestine under the name of "Mary." They saw high, high above her, the eternal feminine prototype of the human soul, which radiates in the Madonna paintings of the high Middle Ages and early Renaissance, giving them their wonderful transparency. These paintings are windows onto a world higher than our own. There is no need to add many words to them.

But are these paintings also a part of the movement that made the soul and everything pertaining to it an end in itself? I would say that Madonna painting was an attempt to protect the Marian mystery from the strictures of dogma. Madonna painting developed quite apart from dogma. In ancient times it was still known that this queen of heaven, this virgin mother, was the very spot in the spiritual universe from which cognitive life was inspired. This knowledge was lost. We might say that from that time on, all fields of study, all science, continued their paths without Mary. But painters and sculptors were still inspired. At least the world now had the divine virgin's gift of beauty and art. Madonna paintings may still be called wisdom's gift. They are wisdom in the form of beauty—beauty as a revelation of cosmic wisdom.

Let us consider as an example the Sistine Madonna by Raphael. At first glance perhaps it does not appear as radiantly beautiful as other paintings of Mary. In this painting, Raphael quite clearly indicates that he was well aware of the connection between Mary and Sophia. The two figures kneeling at the feet of Mary—Pope Sixtus II and St. Barbara—lived in earliest Christian times, and their significance lies precisely in the fact that they were seekers of knowledge, seekers of the spirit. St. Barbara was killed because she had become a pupil of Origen, and hence a Christian, against her father's will. It was her wish to learn, to gain knowledge. She strove to carry Christianity within as gnosis, as spiritual insight, and she was martyred for seeking Christian knowledge.

Pope Sixtus II was also martyred. When he was invited to become bishop of Rome, he was not a Christian yet, but the head of the Philosopher's School in Athens. But, although he was not aware of it, the philosophy he taught contained many Christian elements. That is why, after the death of Origen, those who still wished the practice of Christianity to include the search for knowledge asked him to be bishop of Rome. Raphael's depiction of him as pope is actually historically inaccurate, because he became bishop of Rome before the position of pope existed. And a year after arriving in Rome he was martyred for his belief in a Christianity that includes striving for knowledge.

All this information comes to us from the painting of the Sistine Madonna. Sixtus and St. Barbara are looking up to the Madonna because she is the bearer of the Holy Spirit. Madonna paintings are still illumined by the forgotten spiritual mystery behind the Virgin Mary, either in the transparency of their artistic perfection, or in a more direct fashion. Songs dedicated to the Virgin Mary still contain the same wisdom that lives in fairy tales. Mary is associated with the month of May, with spring, and with the greening of nature. That is the reason for the special services the Catholic Church holds in the month of May. Mary is seen together with the star of Venus in the sky—"Star of the sea, I salute you"—such are the images that still resonate in songs devoted to Mary, so that they speak of more than a self-centered piety of soul and feeling. A hint of the spiritual Mary mystery still radiates out into the soul mystery here.

This movement has long continued to exist apart from official Christianity. I would like to give two examples from within this stream, taken from the writings of Goethe and Novalis. Goethe was still familiar with the Christian mysteries, although he did not want anything to do with the church. When he wants to create a female character, he draws on the mystery of the Virgin Mary more deliberately than most people realize. There is the figure of Iphigenia, whom he characterizes with these words: "All human frailties are atoned for by pure humanity" [or "humanity at its purest and fullest"]. Another of

Goethe's creations is much more characteristic in this connection than is generally known—the seer Makarie in *Wilhelm Meister's Journeyman Years*. Why does Goethe give this mature woman, Makarie, a name that means "soul" in Greek? "Makarismos" means the Beatitudes [*Seligpreisungen*], but the "bliss" in this word does not refer to a selfish, overemotional state. How does Goethe describe this figure? First we have a sentence that is quite reminiscent of Iphigenia: "Everyone felt the presence of a higher being and yet in that presence, they were free to be and act in full accordance with their own natures."

In the presence of such a woman one becomes not only better, but more truly oneself. Next, he touches on the actual Madonna motif: "She remembers that ever since she was a child, her inner self seemed to be permeated by radiant beings, radiant with a light even the brightest daylight could not dim." We could say she is clothed with the sun from her innermost being outward. "Often she would see two suns—one within and the other outside, in the heavens, and two moons, one of which remained the same size throughout all its phases, while the inner moon diminished continually."

Here Goethe is saying that the human organism, insofar as it is soul, has a lunar element living in it, which is like a bowl, a vessel, filled with the content of the sun—a sun spirit within the moon soul. This reminds us of the image of the woman clothed in the sun with the moon at her feet in the twelfth chapter of the Apocalypse. So Goethe is describing Makarie, the seer, as a Madonna—a Madonna still quite within the ancient wisdom tradition.

Novalis brings to life the more-than-earthly beauty of Madonna paintings in poetic form:

A thousand images reveal you,
Mary, in all your loveliness.
And yet there is not one that shows you
The way you live within my soul.

I only know that since I've seen you
The world's confusion is a dream.
I can't express the heavenly sweetness
That's come to live within my soul.

This is the most perfect expression imaginable for what Raphael expressed in his Madonna paintings. Novalis, too, knew about the mystery of Sophia, the mystery of spirit and wisdom behind the inner image of Mary. He brings it to expression at the end of the first section of his novel *Heinrich von Ofterdingen* in this verse:

The Kingdom of eternity is founded,
And every struggle ends in love and peace.
Our dreams of pain and woe are gone at last.
Priestess Sophia rules our hearts for ever.

That is the spiritual side of the Mary mystery, which must shine through the soul-related part.

After taking in all this, we must ask again how the Mary described by Luke—this girl of perhaps twelve or thirteen from Nazareth, who bore a child in a stable in Bethlehem—how this Mary could be an image of wisdom. We readily see her as an image of purity and inner grace, but how can she be an image of wisdom? I think it is of decisive importance today to understand that this Mary was not very clever or intellectual. The important thing about her is the way the spirit lived in her soul. That is why the Gospel of Luke describes this in two places. After the shepherds came to adore the child, Luke says, "Mary kept all these words and pondered them in her heart" (Luke 2:19). And twelve years later, after twelve-year-old Jesus spoke of his experience in the temple, Luke says again, "Mary kept all these words in her heart" (Luke 2:51). So wisdom is created here by meditating on a word; Mary's way of living in the spirit is to hold it in her heart. In this respect, flesh-and-blood Mary may serve as an example to us. She shows us how we can learn to know and see with our hearts again, and thereby do our part to heal human thinking. For in the future, spiritual truths will be of value only if they have first passed through the soul the way the shepherds' words and those of the twelve-year-old Jesus passed through Mary's soul and emerged as radiant wisdom. Only through such objective devotion will humanity be able to find a new wisdom-filled kind of thinking. To allow this to happen, the soul must develop the transparency that allows the spirit to shine through it. The soul must be the moon chalice ready to contain the sun spirit. The spirit soul must carry the soul spirit within it.

Here I may be permitted a few personal words. In 1921, when we were preparing to found the Christian Community, beginning to renew religious life and develop a modern priesthood that could help the world, we thought at first in terms of several years of preparation. But communicating this to Rudolf Steiner, who was advising us along the way, we received this reply, "If you wait any longer, humanity will have forgotten how to think altogether." This surprised us, because it really wasn't our aim to teach a new kind of thinking. We were preparing to re-erect altars and renew the sacraments. But gradually we began to understand that it is the cultic element that renews the ability to concentrate, to worship, and is thus able to lay the foundation for renewed Christian thought and cognition worthy of humanity. Souls must become receptive again; they must acquire Marian capacities.

Sacramental, cultic life is certainly one of the most important tools for raising our fallen thinking and understanding, for bringing wisdom back and allowing Mary Sophia, that divine image inspiring painters and honored in Marian songs, to shine in our souls again. The image of the woman clothed with the sun and standing on the moon and about to give birth to her child—this image must radiate out into our age. For today, the dragon is preparing to devour the child—the child who represents all that we have accomplished in growing towards soul consciousness. Today's Christianity must develop a Christian consciousness and Christian thinking, not just Christian feeling and emotions.

In order to experience the Christ, who has drawn closer to us again, we must transform our consciousness. The first Christ event addressed the *being* of humanity. The second Christ event, which we will soon experience, will address the *consciousness* of humanity. But to experience Christ, mere intellectual consciousness must be raised to a soul-filled spiritual consciousness. This will gradually allow us to feel and to know the sphere in which Christ originates. In this sense, the second Christ event must also inaugurate a new era of the Holy Spirit in humanity. Christianity must again give divine content to our consciousness and bring human knowledge and insight together with feelings of devotion.

3

The Physical Aspect

TODAY WE WILL speak about the most enigmatic, deepest mystery of Mary, the mystery of Marian physicality. Indeed, the dogma of the assumption of Mary, just recently pronounced, has placed the historic, physical figure of Mary in the foreground of Marian devotion. Up to that time, worshippers were still able to see Mary as a window between heaven and earth. They did not necessarily need to fix their gaze on the woman of flesh and blood, incarnated long ago in Palestine; they could see through this figure, sensing behind her the divine soul, the queen of heaven, who revealed herself to the faithful in a variety of images, even in pre-Christian times. But now, due to the new dogma, this figure seems to have been condensed once and for all into the physical figure of Mary. This is not clear at first, since the dogma speaks of physical ascension, assumption—Mary physically received into heavenly glory. Nevertheless, it is the body Mary wore here on earth during her physical incarnation that is being spoken of.

This dogma greatly shocked the rest of the religious world, particularly the Protestants, who were accustomed to keeping spirit and matter quite separate, not only in their worship, but also in their thinking. Over the years they had gotten accustomed to this dualistic worldview, in which spirit and matter are considered almost totally separate, and in which it is deemed unchristian to apply religious feelings and concepts to the physical sphere. And now, suddenly, this dogma places religion squarely on the level of physicality. Indeed, the dogma was even proclaimed to be delivering the final blow to materialism and nihilism. It is quite true that this dogma has tremendous philosophical implications, but it also raises new problems while tacitly creating an obstacle to any real solution of these problems. This dogma raises a question that is of decisive importance to the future of the Christian worldview: Will Christians be bold enough to embrace the view that spiritual forces are able to affect and transform earthly matter, or will they remain mired in abstractions? In response to the new dogma, Catholic scholars have conducted extensive theological and exegetic investigations into this issue, reminding the public that the Protestant creed, too, contains the article about "being raised in the flesh," without Protestants having any clear idea of the relation of spirit to matter. And some Catholic theologians are developing a sort of philosophy by reasoning that Christian redemption applies not only to the human soul, but to the entire human being, including the body. Those of us who work within the Christian Community took this fact as our starting point. Sacrament and transubstantiation—the mystery of the transformation before the altar—only make sense to those who believe that spiritual forces are able to affect material, earthly substance. The Christian Community never questioned this truth, and we would never have begun our work at all if we had not believed that we could incorporate it in our worship. But now, from this Archimedean starting point, the entire materialistic worldview must be transformed. The church cannot start proclaiming the resurrection of the flesh—*resurrectio carnis*—while still believing in a world in which matter is not changed by spirit and spirit is nothing but a joke and unable to have even the slightest effect on the material world.

Important as it is for this issue to be raised at last, it is the cliff on which the bark of Protestant theology will shatter. The only options are to go back to pre-Reformation thinking or to look to the future, to take seriously the perspectives opened up by Rudolf Steiner's work, which enables us to re-approach the deepest mysteries of Christianity through thinking— by means of the inquiring mind. To put it briefly: So far, traditional Christianity, especially Protestantism, has always remained in the realm of the soul. But the soul is able to affect only itself—not the body. Not until we rise from mere soul regions to the reality of spirit do we reach a higher level. At the same time, we also reach a lower level, because spiritual forces are able to affect matter. Spirit in its reality, concretely grasped, will be seen to affect physical substance. But, for the Catholic world, the dogma of 869 blocked any access to actual spirit, to spirit as the highest member of the human organization. According to that dogma, we consist only of body and soul. But if the body can be transformed and actually wrested from death, then surely somewhere there must be spirit at work. According to Catholic thinking, though, this could not be the spirit dwelling in individuals, but only the spirit representing the church. In other words, only the spirit dwelling in the church is able miraculously to affect matter, making possible transubstantiation, resurrection, and assumption.

Here we find ourselves in a strange situation: With transubstantiation and resurrection of the body occurring only as miracles, we are able, while believing in them, to remain complete materialists. For when the assumption of the Virgin Mary is spoken of, at least in popular circles, her body is conceived of in purely physical terms. The official wording of the dogma is more cautious. It keeps the door open to a future spiritual conception as well as to a materialistic conception of Mary, but the church nevertheless condones the way most of the faithful imagine the process—the transformation of the body and blood of Christ is imagined in crude, materialistic terms, even though that is not the official teaching of the church. All of this is quite clear to the attentive observer. According to the most important articles in Catholic journals, especially those written by Jesuits grappling with the new dogma, all of Christianity would be meaningless without a belief in spiritual forces that are able to penetrate the whole human being. Finally, some theologians are beginning to speak in such terms! Regarding the resurrection of the Virgin, they say she is the first example of physical resurrection or assumption. A special act of grace, a special miracle, comes to Mary, allowing her Marian pre-resurrection, assumption, or resurrection of the entire body, such as the rest of humanity will not see until the Last Judgment. There is still a long road ahead before this miracle can be transferred from one single case to humanity as a whole.

Continuing to ponder this issue, theologians run into a roadblock, a seemingly unsolvable problem. The Gospel of Matthew recounts that on Good Friday in the afternoon, when the body of Christ was hanging on the cross, an earthquake opened up the graves and the dead rose up and appeared to the people of Jerusalem. So, according to Matthew, there was physical resurrection even on Good Friday. Suddenly the dead who did not have anything at all to do with Christ rose up out of their tombs. Yet this is crassest materialism! Matthew is not speaking in purely material terms, about graves opening and bones joining together. These are spiritual events, inwardly visible to agitated souls, which actually did flash out over the Golgotha area immediately after the crucifixion. In running into this roadblock, in putting a purely physical interpretation on Matthew, scholars are also devaluing the assumption of Mary as Marian pre-redemption.

The pivotal question is, "How can we truly understand the actual process of the assumption of the Virgin Mary?" We must continue investigating. To this end, I will suggest here, as briefly as possible, how we might gradually arrive at an understanding of the effects of Christ's redemptive act on the human body.

It is a consequence of our materialistic age that when we speak of the human body, we mean only the physical body, the part that is laid in the coffin after death and cremated or buried. The only way to overcome this materialistic view is to find some way to learn of the human body's many layers, either by means of Rudolf Steiner's basic concepts or through some other gradual, careful process. We are made up of more than just our physical body. Our soul does not entirely contain us, either; it is an outer layer, in which our spiritual being lives. And between the soul body and the physical body there is still the life body, woven of the formative forces that keep life in our organism and continually regenerate it. Those who are able to imagine the human body as a triad of soul body, life body, and physical body are already a step closer to being able to imagine that spiritual forces— whether our own alone, or together with higher powers — might affect the physical body. It is obvious that the spiritual forces we carry in us as spiritual ideals directly affect our soul body. The beneficial effects of self-control and systematic inner work are easily imagined and even observed. And this, too, is conceivable that, with the aid of divine grace, the benefits of our inner work might reach deeper and deeper into the human organism. Such spiritual forces ultimately affect not only the soul body, but also the life body and the physical body. We contemporary seekers have a very hard time imagining that spiritual forces might transform solid, earthly matter and even bone. Yet, our physical bodies are more than solid matter; they contain all four elements — the solid, the watery, the gaseous, and the warmth elements. Spirit is able to affect the warmth body (which we also contain) quite easily through the soul. So it really isn't difficult to imagine that spirit might gradually penetrate and transform the physical body.

But, as we have already mentioned, the spiritual part of our nature is actually still hovering above us. The part we call "I" is a temporary, improvised element. Even so, as rudimentary as it might be, the I or ego within us is able to work on these three bodies. And the more it works on them, the more it transforms them, bringing the triad of its own higher being into earthly reality. Humankind, weak and sinful as a result of the Fall, does not have the strength to do this unaided. But if it were possible, through grace and Christ's help, to transform the soul body spiritually, then the soul that leaves the denser bodies at death would no longer be mere soul body—it would be the first redeemed portion of the human organization. It would be spirit soul, called "spirit self" or "Manas" by Anthroposophy. And if it were possible, through the spirit and the power of Christ, to possess, penetrate, and transform the life body, also, then, when the etheric or life body leaves the physical body at death, there would be a transformed, spiritualized etheric body present—a body wrested from death and no longer subject to dissolution. It would be what Anthroposophy calls "life spirit," an expression also found in the letters of St. Paul. And finally, if grace and the spirit should make it possible to permeate the physical body also, then, though the body might be placed in the grave, there would be an imperishable spiritualized physical body present—the result of this spiritualizing process—a body called "spirit man."

I should like to ask you to imagine, in a purely hypothetical way, that long ago there might have been, and in future there might again be, those whose inner sense organs allow them to see what happens on a supersensible level at the moment of death and afterward. They would see in the face of the newly dead not only the physical expression, but also the *source* of the blissful glow often seen there. They would see what has struggled free of the physical body, and witness the beginning of the resurrection and ascension miracles. When Christ died on the cross, there were already some on earth—though perhaps not more than two or three—who were able to see what flowed out of the Redeemer's wounds along with his blood. They could see that a transformed life body had struggled free of the physical form as new, redeemed body, as eternal life. Three days later, on Easter morning, the spirit body, too, rose from the depths of the grave. This was the transformed physical body, a physical spiritual form, a spiritualized physical form. There were also those who were able to witness the spiritual events surrounding the Virgin Mary's death. Some sensed them, some saw them clearly inwardly. Their impressions form the basis of the age-old apostolic legend of Mary's ascension.

Perhaps these completely un-dogmatic reflections may lead to a first intuitive understanding of the miracle of the ascension of Mary.

But now we need to understand how Mary gradually took possession of and permeated the many layers of her physical being over the course of her life. To do this, we must leave abstraction behind and simply listen to the story of her life. However, we will have to start with an account of the two Christmas stories in Luke and Matthew, stressing a fact that many still find surprising, unaccustomed, and even shocking: The two gospels are speaking of two different families and two totally different events that can only be briefly sketched out within the framework of these lectures. The details are available in my book *The Childhood of Jesus*.[2]

The two Christmas stories of the Luke and Matthew

Gospels recount two completely different events. The little child the shepherds worshiped was not the same child to whom the wise men brought their gifts. And, therefore, there were also two Marys. Imagining these stories in the greatest possible detail is a unique opportunity to see destiny at work; nowhere in world history may it be more clearly observed than here.

The Christ mystery swings like a pendulum between the mysteries of the virgin birth and the resurrection. It is possible to be born with virginity remaining from the age of ancient cosmic innocence and harking back to the time when conception and birth were under the influence of the Holy Spirit. This innocence, however, is never "earned"—it is an exceptional gift of karma and nature. Resurrection, on the other hand—and the mystery of ascension is connected with this—can only be gained by inner struggle; that is why we say that Christ *conquered* death. Now, the Church of Rome transferred these two mysteries—that of the virgin birth and that of assumption—from Jesus to Mary. Yet there were two different Marys. The pure virginal soul who tended her child in the manger in the Bethlehem grotto is not the same Mary who stood beside John under the cross and lived in his household in Ephesus. She is not the same Mary whose death in old age was so powerfully experienced by the scattered apostles that they felt themselves to be jointly present with her in the valley of Jehoshaphat. From their experience grew the apostolic legend of the ascension of the Virgin Mary.

These two Mary figures represent a human polarity that is also seen in the two children described in the Christmas gospels.

The child whose birth the Luke Gospel chronicles is an entirely unique child insofar as his birth marks the very beginning of his earthly destiny. Not only does this child have a very young soul; the soul that shines out from him has never before experienced destiny in an earthly body. This child brings down to earth undimmed the heavenly sphere unclouded by the Fall, a circumstance just as unique as that of Christ taking on human form. There never was anything comparable in world history, and there never will be. And the Mary chronicled in the Luke Gospel, the young wife of the carpenter of Nazareth, is inwardly related to this little child, because she, too, is a very young soul. At birth we normally bring the baggage of much history and difficult karma along with us. Those who are familiar with the concept of reincarnation will easily understand this. The soul of the Luke Gospel Mary, however, is pure and heavenly, and thus a fit, pure vessel for the Holy Spirit, radiating the heart wisdom that is a reflection of heavenly light. This young woman, Mary, though not clever or intellectual, has a wise and knowing heart.

The babe that the Matthew Gospel tells of, on the other hand, is not such a young soul. No—he has one of the oldest souls in existence, a most mature soul, bearing tremendous earthly destiny—indeed, formed by this destiny. The three Wise Men from the East, guided by the very being radiating out from the child Jesus, are representatives of the ancient wisdom tradition. They proffer the child their gratitude for the millennia of guidance they have received from him, because this child led and nurtured humanity for millennia. The child's parents are not young, childlike souls, but old and mature. His father, living in Bethlehem, is the son of David and Solomon who would have been king of Israel if Israel had not lost its kingship and its freedom. To those who still believe this dynasty has a future, he is the quiet pretender to the throne of Israel. Therefore, he was not a simple, childlike man like the carpenter of Nazareth; on the contrary, he was the focus of all the leaders of Israel. Mary, who was betrothed to him by the temple priests, was an old soul, as well. She had spent her entire youth as a temple virgin in Jerusalem, and her teachers had been amazed at how her every word surpassed all the world's wisdom. But her words contained more than heart wisdom; they also contained knowledge and thought, formed by a long destiny.

Someday Christians will realize that these two accounts of the Christmas events are entirely different, and that no amount of cleverness will ever be able to reconcile them, because they contain irreconcilable contradictions. And then they will learn to love destiny for having brought together these two streams— the innocent Paradise stream unburdened by karma, and the other, containing the fruits of much karma, many accomplishments, much suffering, and many struggles. So these mysteries of Christ's life, even if only taken in on the level of feeling—that of virginity and of resurrection—really do apply to the two Marys, because the one possesses a virginity so strong that it carries over into motherhood, while the other possesses all the inner qualifications for earning the mystery of resurrection. Or, put a different way, the motherly figure of the Luke Gospel Mary is the personification of the ancient virginity of Paradise, while in the other Mary, we see the possibility of regaining virginity by working our way through the darkness back to the light.

Now we will continue our account of the lives of the two Marys, to deepen our understanding of these issues.

The parents of the pure, childlike Luke Gospel Mary are totally unknown, nameless, plain people, untouched by the life and customs of those days. This also goes for Mary herself. She is much more important as the representative of Paradise than as the daughter of her parents. As the Biblical account begins, she is the wife of a carpenter, also a young, childlike soul, living in a religious Essene community. These two lead a life of loving service. They do not think of themselves and aren't even capable of selfishness yet. Then there is that springtime moment when the Archangel Gabriel appears to Mary. It is his appearance that makes her aware that she has conceived. The spiritual world, the home of the spirit and soul of the child she is to conceive, reveals itself to her in the figure of the Archangel Gabriel, the archangel of birth. And as she becomes aware that she has conceived, the meaning of earthly destiny first touches her pure, paradisiacal soul.

This encounter gives her the impetus to leave her sheltered life in Nazareth and journey to Judea to visit her older relative, Elizabeth. What she witnesses there is strongly karmic and impresses itself deeply on her soul. After a few months, she experiences the birth of John the Baptist to Elizabeth and her husband, Zacharias the priest. Mary's destiny is foreshadowed in the circumstances of their life: Zacharias journeys back and forth between his home in Ain-Kêren and nearby Jerusalem in order to fulfill his priestly duties. Destiny speaks even more strongly when Mary journeys to Bethlehem with her husband Joseph for the census and gives birth to her baby in a grotto that is the site of age-old traditions. These events gradually begin to form an "I" in her pure soul. This is what old Simeon is alluding to in the temple, where the child is presented in accordance with the law, when he says to Mary, "A sword will pierce your soul." No one descends from Paradise to earth without taking on suffering and heavy karmic burdens; the soul finds itself in an entirely different state. Yet we must always remember that original, divine purity never left Mary's heart, even for a moment. She transforms everything that destiny brings her in the light of this wisdom. It is not that she does not feel the pain and the burdens, but she is able to shine a bright golden light on them, because the divine being revered by the ancients as Isis Sophia is able to live in her soul. World wisdom itself pours its golden light into her heart.

In the next twelve years, her son grows up in Nazareth. Mary observes him as he begins to know the earth that is so new to him, passing gradually from a heavenly dream to earthly consciousness. Then new destiny forms as the other family returns from Egypt: the two families begin living together, and the two boys are attracted to each other as with an age-old magnetic force—the very young soul and the very old soul. A polarity of human life begins to resolve. A similar friendship, deep and enigmatic, forms between the two Marys. Outwardly, they are about the same age, but inwardly they embody the polarity of a very young soul and a very old soul. When they converse, it is as if heaven and earth were speaking to each other.

Then, the year the Luke Gospel Jesus turns twelve, that mysterious Eastertide event in Jerusalem occurs: Jesus disappears and is nowhere to be found until, on the third day, his parents come upon him sitting in the temple. He has changed completely. The voice speaking out of him now is that of the other boy. He has not lost the heart wisdom and goodness he got from his mother, but suddenly he can think and say what previously only the other, slightly older boy could. This is a puzzle indeed to his young mother, and at first she has no way of solving it. Significantly, the gospel tells us here that Mary retains and ponders the boy's words in her heart. She does not understand the new language he is speaking, but in taking it up into her heart and letting the golden light of divine inspiration illuminate it, she begins to realize what must have happened. It has to do with the other boy's falling silent from that hour on. He no longer spoke, and in a short time he became ill and died. What had really happened was that the soul of the Luke Gospel child and the strong "I" of the Solomonic child had become one. They had joined and begun to share their substance. This is the event youthful Mary must witness and struggle to understand. But it overwhelms her, and what she does gradually begin to understand bears her away from the earth. This happens at about the same time the other boy dies—perhaps a few days later. It is easy to imagine a connection between the dying souls—that of young Mary and of Solomonic Jesus. They pass into the spiritual world together.

Does this event already contain some of the mystery of Mary's ascension? In a limited way, it does. For her concentrated destiny has formed such a strong "I" in her pure soul that, after her death, or at the moment of death, a kind of ascension is able to take place. A new soul force is formed that does not enter higher worlds after death but is able to continue sharing in earthly events. And that is just the mystery of ascension, that the soul has developed such power that, from heaven, it is able to influence events on earth after death.

Now the life of the Luke Gospel Mary continues in

an altered form in the life of the other Mary. How is this possible? By means of the destiny she has built up through suffering, she is able to share in what happens on earth; she is even able to lend heavenly aid. Here is her son, suddenly so changed. Here is the other Mary, who has lost her son and must now try to fathom this whole strange turn of fate. And the soul of the Mary who has left the earth is able to help and inspire. But it is the being who inspired *her* while she was alive that is really supporting those on earth now—Divine Wisdom herself. And it is this same support that stays with Jesus of Nazareth on all his journeys.

The family of Mary described in the Gospel of Matthew did not live in retirement and obscurity like the family of the Luke Gospel Mary. Her parents' names are very familiar—Joachim and Anna—and these two play an important role in the Apocrypha. They are old and, in view of their age, can no longer expect to become parents. Anna's conception, too, is of a pure nature, the holdover of a more innocent age. The elderly parents consecrate the daughter who has come to them in such an extraordinary, unexpected way to service at the temple. She grows up as a temple virgin from her fourth year on, and all who know her marvel at the understanding, wisdom, and maturity of her soul. She is given in marriage to Joseph of Bethlehem, because the future of her people depends on whether this man, the last representative of a royal line, has a son to rule the kingdom of David when it is brought to life again. That is why

Joseph of Bethlehem is betrothed to this temple virgin and why the birth of their first son naturally draws the attention of all who long for the worldly Messiah, scion of the dynasty of Solomon.

The wise men come to do homage to the babe, but Herod casts a shadow over their visit, and Joseph and Mary set out for Egypt with their child. For several years they live in the ancient sacred city of Heliopolis, where the child and his parents, too, have contact with the Egyptian initiates, the priests of Heliopolis. Though they were no longer influential at that time, and were perhaps quietly living the lives of hermits, they surely retained and imparted much ancient wisdom to the holy family. After returning home, Mary, Joseph, young Jesus, and a second child born in Egypt are swallowed up in the anonymity of Nazareth. These events are all most dramatic, down to their very details. In Nazareth, they are forced to live in very humble circumstances, in the public eye. From now on they live in the Essene colony, where all things are owned in common and a life of poverty without outer possessions is the rule. Nobody knows that they are hiding there. Mary must now accustom herself to an entirely new way of life. This creates destiny, inwardly enriching and maturing her.

In the next few years, she gives birth to several more children. Then the elderly father of this large family dies and Mary becomes a widow. Next, she must cope with the tremendous blow of her son's death, so mysteriously connected with the Easter

event from which the other Jesus emerges transformed. The Luke Gospel Mary dies also. Mary now
has to accustom herself to an unfamiliar way of life
without the aid of her friend. Yet, in mourning the
death of her firstborn, the widow discovers that sorrow makes her more receptive to the help of the
familiar soul of her friend. Though she is no longer
beside her in the flesh, the Luke Gospel Mary is
always present, shining a light of understanding on
the dramatic events of Mary's life. These events, this
destiny, continue to be difficult. Mary forms a very
deep relationship with the son of the Mary who died,
even though she did not give birth to him. This relationship is based on the fact that the ego that she did
give birth to, which was incarnated as her bodily son,
now dwells in the boy who survived. So although she
is not his physical mother, she is his mother in an
inner, deeper sense. Between his twelfth and thirtieth
years, this son passes through deep, formative experiences, which have been described by Rudolf Steiner.[3]

He becomes acutely aware of the way his contemporaries relate to the divine world, recognizing that
ancient religious traditions are dying, that the Jewish
and Pagan religions have no future, and that decadence
is threatening the Essene communities. These three
great disappointments inscribe his heart with pity for
all of humanity. Mary, too, feels all this, because, since
the death of the other Mary, she feels more deeply and
is stronger in heart and soul than before.

When Jesus is thirty, around Christmastime in the

year 30 AD, an event occurs that is of special importance to both Jesus and Mary. Jesus has gathered in all the experiences of alienation from God; he has become their focal point. Now they have ripened in him to the point where he can talk about them to his mother, and he does so in a conversation lasting several days. He seems to be transferring a heavy burden, and as Mary shares it, her whole being changes. This sorrow—not personal sorrow but the sorrow of all humanity—in passing from son to stepmother, now opens up Mary's mature soul, in which so much destiny has already been concentrated, so that the divine soul of Luke's Mary is no longer just hovering over her but is able to unite with her higher being. It is as if the two Marys were becoming one. It is as if this wonderful divine soul originating in Paradise were now incorporated in the ancient soul of Solomonic Mary. And while this is happening, Mary even undergoes a physical transformation. Here we see a human ego so matured by sorrow that it is able to impress its maturity even onto the physical body. But this would not have been possible without the aid of a higher power—the power of love, lending its aid from above, so that, as Steiner has described it, virginity is restored, down to the physical level. Here Mary's biography shows us that spiritual forces are able to transform physical bodies. Paradise is regained, virginity is regained—an inspiring image.

The Mary of Luke's Gospel did not have to struggle to achieve her innocence, which was a gift of nature, and thus she cannot serve as an example to us. But the virginity that the other Mary achieves at the age of forty-four or forty-five through suffering is a goal for all humanity; it was not a gift, but earned. Such images are perhaps more useful in clarifying the difference between one's own effort and grace than theological definitions. The Luke Gospel Mary was the bearer of Divine Sophia, so when her being pours into the other Mary, Divine Sophia enters along with it. From this time on, Mary possesses not only rich life experience, but also divine wisdom, which is able to inspire her every step.

The Christmas season, the holy nights of this particular year—30 AD—are filled with echoes of the conversation between Jesus and his mother. Jesus emerges from these conversations totally changed. He seems to have poured his whole "I" into the exchange, and it is almost as a sleepwalker that he sets out to visit John the Baptist. The journey takes thirteen days. On January 6, he is baptized by John, and, as a result, another transformation takes place in him. The "I" of Christ enters the man Jesus of Nazareth. This transformation is earned rather than received as a gift, because without undergoing suffering first, he could not have become the Christ bearer. Now, both Jesus and Mary have been transformed.

Jesus then gathers the disciples around him. They are to be regarded as the representatives of all humankind, even of those who were not able to follow any of these events. Actually, there was only one disciple who was able to follow every event in the life of Christ, and that was John. Mary is able to be one of the knowing disciples, thanks to the transformation that took place in her during the three years of Christ's life between his baptism and his death on Golgotha. That is why John and Mary are standing beneath the cross alone, while all the others are missing. These two are the ones who have fully shared all of Christ's experiences. They share in the events of the next few days, as well. Mary forms the quiet center of the group of disciples gathered on the morning of Pentecost, on the day when the Holy Spirit began to come to every human being—not, as in earlier times, to women only. Now men, too, share the Holy Spirit's gifts. The presence of Mary is clearly noted in the Acts of the Apostles. Her part in the events of Christ's life is more important, more intensive, than that of any of the disciples with the exception of John, with whom she journeys to Ephesus, where she lives in his household for a number of years.

When she finally returns to Jerusalem in her sixties, destiny again takes her to the temple where she spent her childhood. From her fourth to her twelfth or thirteenth year, she served at the temple. Now she spends her last years in the house of the Coenaculum, where Jesus and his disciples gathered for the last supper, where he appeared to them as the risen one, and where he gathered them on the morning of Pentecost, when the tongues of fire, the Holy Spirit, descended on them. In this house, a home has been made for Mary and here she experiences an "octave" of her temple youth, because this place is, from then on, the new temple.

Finally, the archangel Gabriel foretells her death to her; that is to say, she feels herself beginning to return to the spiritual world and learns the hour of her approaching death. Then, we are told, she calls the twelve apostles scattered over the earth to come to Jerusalem. Hearing her call, they gather in spirit around her deathbed and remain with her in spirit when she dies and until, three days later, she is buried in the Valley of Jehoshaphat. There she is transformed as everyone is transformed three days after death. The apostles see the redeemed part of her soul freeing itself from her physical body. She has shared so fully in the suffering, death, and resurrection of Christ that her soul is totally permeated with his essence, reflecting Christ's life spirit and spirit man. The apostles see a reflection of the transformation that shone forth in full force from the grave on Golgotha. But this is not a miracle; it is the fruit that ripened gradually during the course of a hard, painful destiny. The *mater dolorosa* becomes the *mater gloriosa*, and this transformation, this renewal of virginity, is an ideal, an inspiring image and goal. The Mary mystery has meaning for all of humankind, and a renewed Christian understanding of the human being in its fullest sense will be able to fathom it.

Afterword

Michael Debus

Marian devotion, Mary worship, the cult of the Virgin Mary are often regarded as forms of Catholicism better suited to medieval than to modern times. At best, contemporaries tend to see them as attempts to counterbalance psychologically what is generally perceived as the church's hostility toward women. It is all the more surprising, therefore, that in the midst of our enlightened nineteenth and twentieth centuries the church gave new impetus to Marian devotion with two new dogmas that are anything but easy for our modern minds to grasp. In 1854, Pope Pius IX proclaimed the doctrine of the immaculate conception (*conceptio immaculata*), which freed Mary of original sin. In 1950, Pius XII added, to the dogma of exceptional conception, the dogma of exceptional death—the assumption or physical ascension of the Virgin Mary. It is with near-admiration that we register the courage of the Catholic Church in proclaiming these dogmatic teachings totally unimpressed by the scientific nature of our modern age. Yet we cannot deny that, in its way, the church has acted in accordance with the spirit of the times in setting up these dogmas—for we could characterize our age as a Michaelic age. The twelfth chapter of Revelation contains the images valid for our Michaelic age, which begins in the supersensible world with the defeat of the dragon, the "fall of the spirits of darkness," for which the Archangel Michael was responsible. Michael is also the defender of the great woman of the Apocalypse about to give birth. The drama continues on earth. Rudolf Steiner connected the fall of spirits of darkness with the mid-nineteenth century, which marks the beginning of the Michaelic age.[4] Michael is alive in our time and in the events of our time.

In this age, what we have already become is less important than the *path* that we are taking. Goethe portrayed Faust prophetically as the *striving* man. The concept of inner development is of the greatest importance in the Michaelic age. It is crucial that this process be grasped not just on a material, scientific level, but also on a spiritual level. At its core, that is precisely what Anthroposophy is—a spiritual teaching of evolution—and it is no accident that "Sophia" forms a part of its name. Seen against this background, the two dogmas involving the Virgin Mary seem to have the same goal. Both deal with the issue of inner development so crucial to this age by—quite indirectly—repudiating it. Mary is free of sin and therefore the first representative of humanity to be "completely redeemed" in assumption, physical ascension. The sinless state of the past and the redeemed state of the future meet in her. She is without sin and redeemed at the same time. This means that she cannot travel an earthly path or undergo inner development, because she is "in a state of grace" to begin with.

Today we are confronted with the question of where Michael's quest for wisdom, for Mary-Sophia, is leading humanity. It is important, and characteristic for our time that humanity seeks this wisdom. The sudden popularity of esoteric teachings is only a distorted form of our natural longing for deeper knowledge of higher worlds, for true wisdom. But this Sophia demands schooling, development, inner flexibility, all amounting to real personal growth. Sophia will gain in importance and see "a culmination" of her influence around the turn of the century, as Rudolf Steiner said speaking of Anthroposophy.[5] In his encyclical "Mother of the Redeemer" (*Redemptoris Mater*), which announces a Marian year starting at Pentecost 1987, the present pope makes this connection clear. On the same subject, Cardinal Ratzinger writes that the most important goal of the Marian year is to introduce the Advent season of the year 2000, that important remembrance of the birth of Christ. "In the liturgy of the Church, Advent is the

Marian season, in which Mary offered the Redeemer of the world the shelter of her womb. It is a time filled with expectation and hope. To celebrate Advent means to be filled with Marian spirit."[6] We are indeed in a time of Advent, a Marian or, better yet, "Sophianic" time, as we near the year 2000, and we may be sure that these two Marian dogmas are, in the way already described, pointing to the spiritual position the Catholic Church has adopted in this, the Michaelic age. A *path* to higher wisdom, the development of inner faculties, does not exist for the church.

The foundation for Marian devotion in the church was laid in 431 AD at the third ecumenical council in Ephesus. The place was the great church of the Virgin Mary, not far from the ruins of the Artemis temple, devoted throughout long centuries to keeping alive the mysteries of the great goddess. The council was convened by Emperor Theodosius II for the purpose of deciding if the title "Theokotos" ("God Bearer" or "Mother of God"), originating in Egypt, could rightfully apply to Mary. Cyril, who had been the patriarch of Alexandria since 412, headed those who supported giving her that title. Nestorius, patriarch of Constantinople since 428, headed the other side. He vehemently opposed calling Mary "God Bearer," since, in his opinion, she had given birth only to the man Jesus, who was not filled with the divine Logos until later. This dispute about the nature, the dignity of Mary was basically a Christological issue. How can we conceive of the "human" nature of "divine" logos without losing the unity of the person? This council obscured, even denied, the mystery of Jesus' initial humanity, the fact that Christ was not incarnated in him until he was baptized—a mystery that, up to then, had still been known among churchmen. "Those who say Jesus received his power through the word of God like a human being ... shall be expelled." This was one of the decrees resulting from the council. Cyril emerged victorious; Nestorius was expelled. Steiner once stated that Cyril was "filled with profoundest hatred" toward anything not strictly "Christian and tied to the church." He was not motivated "by a desire for personal power."[7]

Cyril's victory at the Council of Ephesus cleared the way for the rapidly spreading worship of Mary as the God Bearer. Churches were dedicated to her everywhere. Rome, too, now had a church dedicated to her, the Santa Maria Maggiore, erected on the foundations of the temple of Kybele dedicated to the Pagan mother of God. In Mary, Christendom worshiped the being who had endowed the Logos with humanity. Christ had become man *ex Maria virgine*. Over the centuries, Christ, in his divine glory and in his role as the stern judge of the world, began to seem more and more remote, and Mary, in her human accessibility, gained in importance. To the faithful, she became "totally pure" and free of original sin (*immaculata*), a mediator (*mediatrix*) whose intercessions became a way to Christ. She even became the "co-redeemer" (*corre-demptrix*), the "completely redeemed" (*assumpta*)—

redeemed by Christ ahead of the rest of humanity. And finally, she became the "new Eve," the mother of humanity redeemed.

In the image of Mary, human nature is experienced as *feminine* and therefore one-sidedly "receptive," which led to serious consequences: Several images merged in a fateful way. From earliest times—as far back as the time of Theodosius—Mary was seen as *typus ecclesiae*, as a symbol of the Christian church, which receives in its midst Him in Whose name all are gathered. The human nature of the Logos, as developed through Marian devotion, could thus be transferred to the Church. She was now able to be "co-redeemer," which influenced the Catholic view of the role of the sacraments particularly. The church always remains pure (as Goethe's Mephisto puts it, she can even "stomach wrongfully-gained riches"). The kingdom of God on earth is already a reality (*assumpta*) within her. She is the essential mediator, "the only road to salvation." Not until this point had been reached did it become possible for the priests to widen their roles as mediators to the wielding of churchly power. The only way those who have begun to form independent religious views and to claim spiritual autonomy can be saved from their error is to *return* to the "bosom of the church" like an "obedient child," because the only way to relate to a *mother* is as a *child*.

The Reformation, a rebellion of the newly autonomous against the Middle Ages, was bound by its innermost impulses to break with the tradition of

Marian devotion. Characteristically, it led to a discovery of Jesus the *man*. Now, the human component of the Logos was no longer just the Virgin Mary, the feminine, and thus churchly. The goals and image of the church changed radically, taking on a form better suited to the new inner autonomy of the faithful. But still the Reformation was missing the "spear point" of true spiritual insight, so that after several centuries it began to crumble from within.

The Christian Community, considered by its founders to be "the third church," does not practice Marian devotion, because it shares the view put forth by Nestor at the Council of Ephesus. Jesus was not *born* the Redeemer and Son of God. The Christian Community creed says, "In Jesus, Christ entered as man into the earthly world." This was accomplished by Christ's baptism in the Jordan, during which a voice from above said, "You are my beloved son…" But this event did not secure and guarantee the work of redemption, either. Even the Son of God had to struggle to achieve his purpose. The ancient church, however, could not conceive of "a struggling God," and that is why, at the First Ecumenical Council in Nicaea in 325 AD, it was proclaimed that the Logos was redeemer from the outset, and thus did not have to undergo inner development. The formulation "The son is *identical* [and not just similar] to the father" expressed this view. As a result of this decree, the conception of Christ began to move closer to that of the Council of Ephesus, where, as already indicated, the church took another big step toward making Christ the remote world judge whom the faithful found hard to approach. A mediator was now needed, and that role fell to the Virgin Mary. Today, Christ may be experienced in a totally different way. As Michael Bauer put it, "Christ is the truest home we have in this world." Today, however, many feel they need a mediator to reach Christ, who himself has always mediated between us and God the Father: "No one can come to the Father except through me." This indicates that any clear distinction between father and son was lost a long time ago.

Another reason Marian devotion is not practiced in the Christian Community has to do with its new conception of the *human nature* of the Logos. The relevant passage in the Creed states, "The birth of Jesus on earth is a working of the Holy Spirit who, to heal spiritually the sickness of sin within the bodily nature of mankind, prepared the son of Mary to be the vehicle of Christ." The "vehicle of Christ," the being enabling Christ to incarnate, is *masculine.* Our attention is now focused not on Mary (*ex Maria virgine*) but on Jesus. (This statement, while it corrects the Council of Ephesus' conception of the human nature of the Logos, also contains the only mention of Mary in Christian Community liturgy). There are basic differences between the masculine and the feminine, and they are not the differences between man and woman, but certain qualities found in both. The "mother" is the archetypal foundation of our earthly existence.

When we "return home" for new strength, our mother awaits us there. She does not judge; she nurtures and cares for her children, and her love encompasses them all. Our father does not wait for us at home. On the contrary—he leaves home every morning to return in the evening, bringing new experiences with him. As the children grow up, this example endows them with the strength to leave home and become independent some day, too. The father's relationship with his children is different from the mother's. All children are alike to her, but not to him, and he might even have a "favorite."

The feminine and the masculine may be seen as basic impulses of a polar nature, one "generalizing," the other "individualizing." At a childlike stage, humankind needs mothering, needs a place to return to again and again after small, often painful, forays into individualization. On reaching maturity, however, humanity seeks the masculine powers of individualization that make possible the necessary break with the past and the search for a new "home." Knowing this, we realize how important it is that the human nature of the Logos, the "vehicle of the Christ," be seen as *masculine* today, in direct polarity to the way it is seen in the Council of Ephesus, and that this is the conception of Christ conducive to our striving for autonomy.

This insight enables us to look at Mary in entirely new ways. There is a subtle reference to this in the passage from the Creed cited earlier. The Holy Spirit not only brings about the birth of Jesus; it also "prepares" the "son of Mary" to receive the Christ. Higher guidance actually does prepare Jesus, creating a *path* that leads him to the Jordan's shore. It is the masculine path of individualization leading to the true ego. The gospels do not speak of this path which Jesus walked during those eighteen years between his twelfth and thirtieth years. It is one of the central achievements of Anthroposophy to have discovered and described these events, and they make possible an entirely new way of relating to the Virgin Mary, for Jesus is only able to walk this path as the "son of Mary." It includes outer journeys to a great variety of places and leads Jesus to form a comprehensive diagnosis of humanity's spiritual state: The last remaining ties with the divine world have been broken. Spiritual development is at an end. All have "lost their divine nature" (cf. the Creed) and their souls are threatened by death. Jesus shares this experience with his mother. Rudolf Steiner gives us an account of the deep, comprehensive exchange between them at the end of those eighteen years, which may well have been a summary of other conversations that took place at intervals during this period. The son unburdens himself; his mother listens. She listens in a particular, entirely nonjudgmental way. This way of listening is crucial to the process, and quite unimaginable today, since we are always forming immediate opinions on what we hear.

Luke tells us twice how Mary receives words she does not immediately understand: "Mary kept all these words and pondered them in her heart." It is the same quality Christ refers to in the parable of the four kinds of soil [the parable of the sower, Mk 4:1-9]: One seed falls on the roadway, one onto the rocks, one among thorns, and the last into good soil, and that, alone, is able to grow. Luke tells us, "The seed is the word of God." The good earth gives shelter to the word. That is why Mary is thought of as "the good soil." The word able to grow in her is not that of quick, logical judgment. There are truths that cannot be fathomed by mere thought; they must be allowed to ripen in the soul slowly, patiently, until they blossom as wisdom. Yet living with what one does not understand is sometimes painful. This kind of suffering [*Leiden*] becomes compassion [*Mit-leiden*] when it is shared. What Mary's son tells her about humankind's situation raises the deepest compassion in her, even before she has understood it. Yet in "keeping and pondering" what she did not understand, she is *gaining wisdom through compassion* (a lapidary, mysterious formulation found in Wagner's *Parsifal*).

Jesus seems to have emptied himself out in telling all this to his mother. The future seems to hold no solution, and his diagnosis begs the question of healing. Mary has taken in her son's words, patiently retaining and pondering them. And thus, step by step, the answer begins to come to her. "Becoming wise through compassion," she finds her soul filling with Sophia, who becomes her higher being, and she understands the mystery of Jesus Christ.

Certain Old Testament passages may help us

understand what happens during baptism. In Proverbs and the Wisdom of Solomon there are indications of Sophia's (Wisdom's) role in Creation: "The Lord created me at the beginning of his work, the first of his acts long ago. Ages ago I was set up, at the first, before the beginning of the earth... When he prepared the heavens I was there ... when he appointed the foundations of the earth, then I was beside him ... and was daily his delight, rejoicing before him always." Then: "For she [Wisdom] is the reflections of eternal light, a spotless mirror of the working of God, and an image of his goodness."[8] Sophia existed before the rest of creation, as a mirror into which God gazes as he creates. She is the feminine in its highest mythical form. The masculine creator must recognize himself in the mirror of the feminine before he is able to begin his work. These passages help us to understand the events following the baptism; there are some parallels between them: The actions Christ Jesus performs together with his mother are possible only because "Sophia," pure mirror of the Creator, has incarnated in her. In Christ's baptism, we see the prototype of St. Paul's mystical insight of "not I, but the Christ in me." Regarding the future of humankind, Christ has totally "out-spoken," "expressed" himself. In his emptiness, all he can say is "not I." At that moment, his "I" seems to leave him. John baptizes him and the Son of God enters him in the image of a dove: "...but the Christ in me." The Logos, the divine, creative word, becomes man.

In the outer world of the senses, the Logos has totally expressed, exhausted itself [*sich erschöpft*]; it has reached its end. But the process of creation may now continue within humanity. The Gospel of John recounts seven signs performed by Christ. They are the prototypes of a new week of Creation, the beginning of the Son's creation, issuing from the Father's completed creation. The first of these signs, performed at the wedding at Cana, marked the beginning of this creative period, but not only its outer beginning. The Greek word used here—*arché*—means more than "beginning," as indicated by the Latin translation *principium*. So this first miracle is the principle of all seven signs. It is of *principal* importance that the mother of Jesus be present here. Key to Christ's creative act, that of turning water into wine, is his conversation with his mother. They continue on a higher level what was of such basic importance during the previous eighteen years. But now it is Mary Sophia in whose mirror Christ's creative power awakens; this is similar to the Old Testament's description of Yahweh's creation. New creation springs up through the interaction between the incarnated Logos and incarnated Sophia. The creation here begun is completed on Golgotha. The crucified Christ's lasts words are, "It is accomplished" (*tetelestai*) or "The goal has been reached."

This goal is linked with a very particular act: The creative power of the Logos is transferred to humankind. John, the disciple whom the Lord loved, is standing beneath the cross as a representative of humanity. The mother of Christ, Mary Sophia, is standing there, as well. The words of the Crucified One—"Behold your mother—behold your son"— bring them together. Humankind now takes over the role the Christ-Logos occupied in relation to Sophia. It is we who are charged with continuing the new Creation. John takes Sophia "unto himself" (*eis taidia*); he identifies with her and makes her wholly a part of his being. Creative will and creative thought join to form the image of the free, autonomous men and women of the future.

In this succession of images, Mary moves early on from the role of mother to that of the man's feminine partner in conversations and creative acts. Correspondingly, Jesus moves from the role of a son to that of a partner. This partnership between the Christ-Logos and Mary Sophia becomes even clearer in the creative acts arising from them. The same relationship is forecast by pre-Christian myths. In Egyptian mythology, for example, the primal constellation is Osiris (the father), Isis (his wife), and Horus (their son). But in the sun's course, after twenty-four hours, their images blend. The god of the sun is "at once son (as Horus) and husband (as Osiris) of Isis (his wife)."[9] Thus, Isis is shown to be both mother and wife of the sun god. Inner images of Mary, formed in modern consciousness, are quite similar: Mary is not a motherly being existing outside of us, to whom we may turn in childlike prayer and special forms of worship; she appears as mother and wife at once, as the "eternal feminine," as Sophia *within* us, whenever, in striving for freedom, we are freeing our inner creativity. For us, today, such striving means conversation "with ourselves." Its prototype is the conversation of Christ with the mother able to be a pure mirror, the "principle" of his creative acts, beginning with the miracle performed at Cana. Similarly, Sophia is also our inner mirror into which we must gaze to make this inner dialogue, the beginning of creativity, possible.

These important inner dialogues do not take place during our waking hours, but in nighttime dream consciousness. Retrospection, a review of our actions and experiences, and resolutions for the coming days play an important role in the "nighttime conversations" we hold with our "mother" and mirror Sophia. These are conversations with the angel hierarchies from whom we seek knowledge about moral issues and the identity of our true ego. Cultivating this relationship with "mother" night, we are creating modern Marian devotion, which is at the same time a path to inner freedom. When the soul is properly prepared for sleep, a wide range of possibilities opens before us. Just as Jesus' conversations with his mother prepared him to take on the being of Christ in the Jordan River, sleep experiences and dialogues with night wisdom may form stations on the quest for our true ego. This newly achieved relationship with the night may be considered appropriate Marian devotion for our day.

Thus, today's Marian devotion becomes a reversal of medieval Mary worship, because it strives for inner autonomy. Yet, at the same time, it enables us to recognize more fully than ever the wonderful inner images of traditional Marian devotion. Modern consciousness is able to affirm them in a new way. Emil Bock's profound lectures do this for us, retaining their full validity even after almost fifty years.

Notes

1. Emil Bock, *Childhood of Jesus*, Edinburgh: Floris Books.

2. Rudolf Steiner, *Cosmic Memory*, Blauvelt: Garber Publications; *The Fifth Gospel*, London: Rudolf Steiner Press.

3. Rudolf Steiner, *Cosmic Memory*, Blauvelt: Garber Publications; *The Fifth Gospel*, London: Rudolf Steiner Press.

4. Rudolf Steiner, *The Fall of the Spirits of Darkness*, London: Rudolf Steiner Press .

5. Rudolf Steiner *Karmic Relationships*, Vol. 6,. London: Rudolf Steiner Press.

6. Joseph Ratzinger, *Mary: God's Yes to Man*, San Francisco: Ignatius Press.

7. Rudolf Steiner, *Occult History*, London: Rudolf Steiner Press.

8. Proverbs 8:22-31, Wisdom of Solomon 7:26.

9. F. Teichmann: *Der Mensch und seine Tempel, Ägypten*. Stuttgart: Verlag Urachhaus.